Panther Chameleon Care Handbook:

Complete Guide on Panther Chameleon Nurturing; Conduct, Health Issues, What They Eat, Lodging & Picking One as a Pet, Things to Know Before Purchase, Etc.

By

Mitchell T. Cudmore

TABLE OF CONTENTS

CHAPTER 1

INTRODUCTION

Panther chameleons show a wide range of splendid shading transforms or stages named after the geographic area they come from in their local environment of Madagascar.

Females show less variety in shading (frequently orange or tanish) and have a less emotional "protective cap" than guys (included edges at the edges of the head), just as being more modest.

Breed Overview

Basic Name: Panther chameleon

Logical Name: Furcifer pardalis

Grown-up Size: Panther chameleons can reach up to or around 21 creeps long; albeit those in bondage will in general remain somewhat more modest (this incorporates the tail). Guys are much greater than female counterpart.

Future: Approximately 5 years in imprisonment.

Trouble of Care: Easy

CHAPTER 2

CONDUCT AS WELL AS TEMPERAMENT OF PANTHER CHAMELEON ONE SHOULD UNDERSTAND

Conduct and Temperament

Panther chameleons are regional and ought to be housed exclusively. Taking care of will in general be upsetting, so likewise with different chameleons, they are pets that are more qualified to being observed as opposed to being taken care of.

Panther chameleons, as most different types of chameleon, are regional; if two guys are housed together in imprisonment, they change tone and now and again assault one another. In the wild, this is important for the custom of guys picking female mates.

These reptiles have astoundingly long tongues, with which they can grab their prey out of mid-air.

They don't live extremely long in bondage, yet they for the most part have compliant disposition and the reality is that they're moderately simple to really focus on contrasted with different reptiles make panther chameleons a top pick among reptile proprietors.

CHAPTER 3

LODGING THE PANTHER CHAMELEON AS WELL THE REQUIRED ATMOSPHERE IT NEEDS

Lodging

Panther chameleons ought to never be housed in glass terrariums. They need the ventilation given by a cross section of fenced area. Fine metal or fibreglass network isn't suggested for chameleon nooks; PVC covered equipment fabric is acceptable.

Vertical space is fundamental to permit the chameleon to climb, and a confine size of a day and a half by 24 crawls by a day and a half 48 inches tall is suggested (the greater and taller the better—chameleons like to move high up off the ground). An open air confine can be utilized when the climate is sufficiently warm, insofar as overheating is forestalled.

Give loads of solid non-harmful plants and branches. Ficus trees have regularly been utilized in chameleon lodging, yet require some alert as the sap can be bothering. Different plants you could attempt incorporate pothos, hibiscus, and dracaena. Fake plants may likewise be added, and counterfeit plants are an incredible option. A decent determination of parts of various breadths ought to be given, ensuring there are secure roosts at various levels and temperatures inside the pen.

Substrate

Neatness in the enclosure is crucial to forestall bacterial or shape development. Utilizing paper towels or paper to line the pen makes cleaning most straightforward. Pruned plants can be put on a plain paper substrate for simpler cleaning while as yet permitting live planting in the enclosure. Try not to utilize wood chips or whatever other substrate that could be incidentally ingested and cause blockages.

Temperature

A daytime temperature slope of somewhere in the range of 75 and 90 degrees ought to be given, with a lolling spot at 95 degrees, around evening time, the base temperature ought not to drop in excess of 15 degrees. Warming is best cultivated by a luxuriating or glowing light in a reflector or a fired warmth component, any of which ought to be put outside of the pen to forestall consumes.

Lighting

Chameleons need a bright (UVA/UVB) light source, so put resources into a decent bulb, for example, the Zoomed Reptisun 5.0. Keep the UV light on for 10 to 12 hours out of every day. Recall these bulbs should be supplanted at regular intervals. Chameleons additionally take an advantage from investing energy outside in normal daylight when the temperatures are suitable (yet be careful with overheating—ensure conceal is consistently accessible).

Moistness

Panther chameleons need a high moistness level; it's ideal to focus on somewhere in the range of 60 and 85 percent. This can be cultivated by clouding the plants routinely, and a trickle or moistening framework is likewise suggested.

Chameleons once in a while drink from a water bowl, however they will slurp up drops of water off plants, so the moistening/trickle framework likewise fills in as a water source. Position a dribble framework so the water beads course over the plants in the walled area. Put resources into a hygrometer to quantify moistness.

CHAPTER 4

PANTHER CHAMELEON DIETS YOU SHOULD KNOW NOW

Food as Well as Water

Panther chameleons are insectivores so ought to be taken care of with an assortment of bugs. Crickets are generally the pillar of the eating routine; however insects, cockroaches, spread worms (useful for calcium), silkworms, flies, and grasshoppers can be taken care of, just as mealworms, super worms, and wax worms.

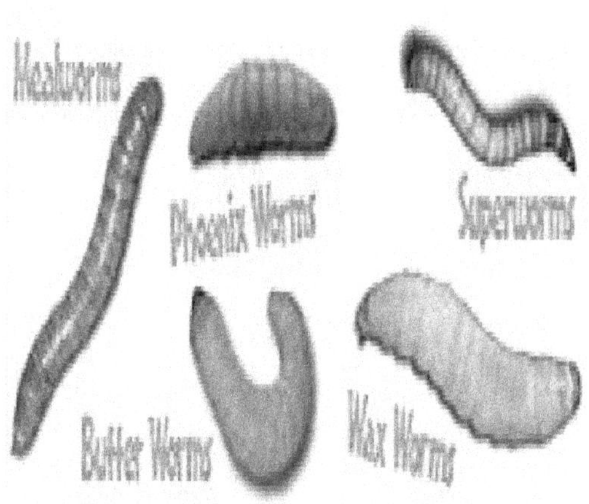

Be careful about wild-got creepy crawlies because of conceivable openness to pesticides and stay away from fireflies.

All creepy crawlies ought to be gut stacked (took care of new veggies and nutrient/minerals) prior to taking care of. Moreover, a few chameleons will likewise eat a touch of plant matter, including collard greens; mustard greens, turnip greens, and sugar snap pea pods.

In the event that you find uneaten bugs or your chameleon is by all accounts acquiring a great deal of weight, you can scale back the sum you're taking care of, or how frequently you feed it. Also, make sure to never leave live prey in the enclosure for expanded periods as creepy crawlies may assault the chameleon.

Make a point to gut load your creepy crawlies well, and it's judicious to clean bugs with a calcium/nutrient D3 supplement (for example Rep-Cal) a few times each week and utilize a wide nutrient mineral enhancement once every week. A few specialists suggest picking an enhancement that doesn't contain nutrient A (utilization beta-carotene all things considered).

CHAPTER 5

CHOOSING ONE'S PANTHER CHAMELEON PLUS COMMON HEALTH CHALLENGES YOU SHOULD KNOW

Picking Your Panther Chameleon

Search for a chameleon whose eyes are clear, and who doesn't give the indications of a respiratory disease: trouble breathing or wheezing, laziness and an absence of craving. On the off chance that it has dry skin fixes, that might be an indication of a parasitic disease.

Likewise with every intriguing pet, the most ideal choice is a respectable raiser who represents considerable authority in reptiles.

Regular Health Problems

Calcium and nutrient A insufficiencies are normal among chameleons including the panther. This condition is normally the after-effect of a horrible eating routine.

Also, as other chameleon breeds, panthers are inclined to mouth decay, or stomatitis, a contamination around the mouth that shows redness and overabundance salivation or slobbering.

Maybe the most genuine ailment for hostage chameleons is the metabolic bone infection. This condition, which can be deadly if not treated in an opportune design, makes a chameleon's bones become frail and weak. A chameleon with this illness will seem torpid and may lose their hunger.

Similarly as with any condition where your pet appears to be sick or pushed, counsel a veterinarian who represents considerable authority in reptiles.

CHAPTER6

PROS AS WELL AS CONS OF KEEPING PANTHER CHAMELEONS

The advantages and disadvantages of keeping a Chameleon as a pet

Chameleons are a kind of old-world reptiles. Their tones differ generally as indicated by their territory and they have the capacity to change tones. As the chameleon skin is comprised of four distinct layers in particular epidermis, chromatophore, melanophore, and under layers, and these layers contain diverse shading colours in their forms; diverse shading designs are showed when these layers contract or grow in the occasions of being terrified by something like light and temperature or feelings related during or after a tussle with another chameleon. Their noticeable highlights are zygodactylous feet which represent the toes of each foot to be intertwined in gatherings of two and three then again in the front and rear feet for improving handle of the tree limbs, since a long time ago collapsed and tacky shot tongue to get prey from good ways, and a couple of freely turning eyes which adds to their sharpness yet are engaged as one while getting their prey.

They generally live in the tropical rainforests, African deserts, South Asian level, and Southern

Europe's savannah, yet they are liked by numerous individuals as pets and they are found in family limits in numerous pieces of the world.

The Pros:

They are cute: They look pretty excellent and the way that they can change tones which makes them cuter.

They are low-energy pets: Chameleons are sluggish and low-energy creatures. They generally live joyfully inside their natural surroundings comprised of plants and branches which they can jump on, gave the sort of food they lean toward is additionally kept in the enclosure. A few group lean toward them as a pet since they possess more energy for their standard exercises. Just once their pen or terrarium is set up appropriately along the essential rules and from that point forward, it is just to be checked so the provisions are appropriately kept up.

They live more: Chameleons by and large live in the wild for simply 2 to 3 years. In any case, if legitimate consideration is taken by the proprietors, they can satisfy 10 years which is a significant long an ideal opportunity for a pet to remain around.

They weigh less: The heaviness of a chameleon varies from one animal group to another. It likewise varies as per the age and soundness of the reptile. The heaviness of a male hidden chameleon shifts from 85 grams to 170 grams, though that of a female hidden chameleon drifts between 85 grams and 118 grams.

Quiet animals when left alone: The chameleons are extremely quiet animals. In the event that they are given legitimate sustenance and a territory like theirs where they used to live, they will remain reasonably bright and won't inconvenience you in any way.

They are warm: They are friendly as in they need appropriate consideration concerning the territory and food that they are utilized to, and as long as these two things are given appropriately, they won't care about your friendship and won't tear into you.

The Cons

Personal stench: Chameleons don't have any scent all things considered however smell like spoiled meat when they wipe their jaws against tree limbs radiating a noxious, waxy material to draw in prey. In addition, the chameleons discharge white shaded crap which scents like human pee somewhat.

Medical problems: Much consideration is to be taken to guarantee that the territory of the chameleon is totally kept up. In any case, various medical problems can come up like Edema, Injuries, Respiratory Infection, Shedding, Mouth Infection, Tongue Retraction Problem, and Egg Binding.

Temperature Adaptability: Different sorts of chameleons lean toward various temperature ranges. So legitimate consideration must be taken to check with a thermometer that the temperature is inside the reach. Something else, a little sprinkling of water must be done or some additional luxuriating bulbs are to be lit. By and large, the temperature range that the majority of the chameleons can bear is 50 degrees Fahrenheit to 70 degrees Fahrenheit.

Diet Needs: Chameleons are insectivorous reptiles. Bugs like crickets, mealworms, wax worms, and super worms are to be gut stacked first with nutritious food, and afterward they are to be taken care of with regard to the chameleon. Pinkie mouse, an infant mouse, can be taken care of to an enormous chameleon pet. Plants like mustard, collard, romaine lettuce, kale, turnip, and dandelion greens can be cleaved to more modest sizes and gave. Reptile supplements like Calcium with Vitamin D3 and Multivitamins are accessible as powder, which is to be sprinkled in ideal sums on the food to forestall Vitamin A, Calcium and Vitamin D3 lacks. Water must be given through a mister or a dripper or a splash bottle gradually so beads structure on the leaves where from the chameleon can drink water.

Extraordinary Lighted Environment: The chameleons are extremely quiet animals. In the event that they are given appropriate sustenance and environment like theirs where they used to live, they will remain reasonably bright and won't inconvenience you in any way shape or form.

Value: The expense of a chameleon fluctuates from one animal type to another. The expense of a pet veiled chameleon in the US market shifts from $30 to $100 contingent upon the age and soundness of the reptile. In any case, the expense of making its environment and keeping up, it is really high.

The facts confirm that every one of us may have our own viewpoint when concluding whether to receive a chameleon as a pet. This amazing guide has attempted to weigh out the two sides of the coin dependent on popular assessment and intelligent significance. Look at which you can identify with most and likewise settle on your choice.

CHAPTER 7

UNIQUE FACTS TO KNOW BEFORE PURCHASING YOUR PANTHER CHAMELEONS

Things to Know Before Buying a Chameleon

Chameleons are dazzling animals that can change tone, move their eyes freely of one another, and get prey with their long, tacky tongues. It is no big surprise that so many are quick to keep these extraordinary reptiles as pets.

On the off chance that you are thinking about offering a home to a chameleon, remember that these reptiles have one of a kind natural surroundings and taking care of necessities that make them more hard to really focus on than some other little or fascinating pets. We should take a gander at five significant interesting points prior to purchasing a chameleon.

I.

Chameleons Need Specialized Housing

This reptile requires explicit conditions to remain solid and glad; thusly giving an appropriate confine arrangement is very difficult.

Chameleons live in the trees, which imply their tall fenced area should incorporate an enormous number of branches and plants to give the thick foliage that these reptiles have in their characteristic living spaces. Doing this assists them with having a sense of safety, offers them a chance to investigate and stow away, and limits pressure.

An ordinary arrangement ought to in any event 3 x 3 x 4 feet. In a perfect world, the enclosure ought to be tall and situated higher up (like on a table, instead of on the floor). This will assist your chameleon with having a liked, more raised vantage point.

Branches and plants are not everything necessary. Chameleons additionally require additional provisions like an UVA/UVB light source, thermometers, mugginess checks, and sirs or trickle frameworks.

These additional provisions can undoubtedly accumulate in cost, so make certain to compute how much your ideal arrangement will cost. Some can get very expensive.

II.

Chameleons Require Live Food and Regular Misting

A basic food dish and water bowl will not work for this colourful pet. Similarly as their enclosure should be as near their normal living space as could really be expected, so should their food and water supply.

Chameleons eat an eating routine of live gut-stacked bugs. This implies you should have an inventory of crickets, mealworms, or wax worms available. Also, you may have to tidy the bugs with enhancements to guarantee that your chameleon is getting every one of the supplements they need to remain solid.

With respect to water, chameleons drink from water beads that gather on leaves. Consequently, normal moistening is needed to guarantee your chameleon is appropriately hydrated. This should be possible by hand; however programmed sirs can likewise be utilized.

III.

Chameleons Are Not Cuddly Pets

Chameleons are singular creatures that don't care for much taking care of or organization. As a rule, it is vital that you house just a single chameleon to forestall battles and stress. Guys can be especially rough to different guys.

Chameleons are somewhat quiet creatures when in singular settings, notwithstanding. They are sluggish and interesting to watch.

Chameleons are not exceptionally vocal about disdaining a circumstance. At the point when a chameleon is focused on it will no doubt freeze or open its mouth, yet it doesn't lash out or wriggle. Hence, when unpractised chameleon proprietors attempt to deal with their chameleons and see this conduct, many can mistake it for acknowledgment as opposed to pressure. Learning a chameleon's propensities and nature can help you appropriately read indications of pain or joy.

IV.

A Good Cage Cleaning Routine is Required

Similarly as with any creature that lives inside a confine, there are cleaning prerequisites. To keep your chameleon sound and glad, there are basic cleaning schedules that should be possible every day, just as more profound cleanings week by week and yearly.

For day by day cleaning, a straightforward spot clean is ideal. Eliminate any dead bugs or crap and wipe down any obstinate regions.

Consistently, you should clear out the confine all the more completely, including a speedy wipe-down of the plants and branches inside the enclosure.

At any rate once each year, it is ideal to move your chameleon to a protected, secure region so you can totally dismantle the enclosure. This permits you to splash any branches or adornments, altogether wipe plants, and wash within the enclosure.

V.

Chameleons Can Easily Become Stressed

Chameleons are exceptionally helpless to pressure, yet their showcases of nervousness can without much of a stretch be missed or misconstrued. It is vital to have the option to comprehend when your chameleon is restless since raised feelings of anxiety can make these pets more inclined to sickness or infection. You ought to likewise limit dealing with and changes in the climate.

You should purchase a chameleon brought up in bondage, instead of endeavour to tame a wild-got chameleon. Chameleons, when all is said in done, don't adjust well to imprisonment or changes in their current circumstance, and this is particularly valid for wild-got chameleons that are constrained into another, hostage climate. On top of this, wild-got chameleons can likewise have other medical issues, like parasites.

Female chameleons can be inclined to additional pressure from egg-laying and might be more inclined to disorders. Male chameleons generally live more.

Other regular medical problems for chameleons may incorporate calcium and nutrient A lacks, stomatitis, and metabolic bone infection.

A chameleon's consideration necessities are more itemized than numerous different pets. In this way, the choice to bring one into your home ought to be painstakingly assessed.

Nonetheless, with the legitimate information and arrangement, chameleons can be incredibly pleasant pets that offer unlimited measures of miracle to your day by day life.

CHAPTER 8

CONCLUSION

Having gone through the nitty-gritty of panther chameleon; I am sure you will stick to the guidelines of caring/ for your amazing chameleon.

Keep in mind; there no shot-cuts to caring for your new pet (Panther Chameleon).

Happy pet nurturing!

THE END.

www.ingramcontent.com/pod-product-compliance
Ingram Content Group UK Ltd.
Pitfield, Milton Keynes, MK11 3LW, UK
UKHW021934190726
13853UKWH00004B/1436

9 798515 840921